Temptation of Wood

Nancy Byrne Iannucci

Nixes Mate Books
Allston, Massachusetts

Copyright © 2018 Nancy Byrne Iannucci

Book design by d'Entremont
Cover photograph by Paul Brookes

All rights reserved. This book or any portion thereof may not be reproduced or used in any manner whatsoever without the express written permission of the publisher except for the use of brief quotations in a book review or scholarly journal.

ISBN 978-0-9993971-8-3

Nixes Mate Books
POBox 1179
Allston, MA 02134
nixesmate.pub/books

Dedicated to love, nature, myth, music, and magic.

Contents

Traffic	1
A Flower in a Frost Cover	2
Taxis to Nowhere	5
Ischia	6
The Neighbors	10
Chicken Soup	11
The Way I Was	12
The Day After	15
The White Building	16
Target Rock, 1983	18
Diggum	20
Go-Go Boots	22
Vicious Cycle	24
Wild Woman	26
Ophelia's Stepsister	28
Castlerigg Circle	30
Raven	33
Sea Bush	34
Sex in the Sky	36
Cattails	39

My Love in Ring Years	40
My Trees at Dusk	44
Hydrangeas	46
Asintmah's Warning	48
Howling	50
Women of the 16th Century	52
An Ode to Aurora	54
Illusionist	56

Temptation of Wood

Traffic

Stained glass street lamps guide travelers through dense frankincense. The eastbound lane passes fourteen rest-stops of condemnation, whores, & afflicted mothers visible only to those rubbernecking. They reach their destination by the shore & watch their children in white diving head-first into pools of oily rejuvenation, trusting they'll lead lives free of temptation. The westbound lane moves at a 6 pm Long Island Expressway pace en route to the city; as they inch closer & closer they question & curse their plight; they blast their horns in tears. The long wait to their destinations, to their homes, to their loved ones seem like centuries to bear after a long day. The heat of the afternoon singes their black clothing through the sun glaring glass. As they exit the tunnel passing the entering eastbound traffic, they both dip their fingers into the holy water.

A Flower in a Frost Cover

*I live
like a hobbit
in a hole,* he said,
the day I thought
he was dead.

He
staggered out
into the blizzard with his
burly aching feet,
wearing

no
shoes, no
pants, no shirt,
only boxer shorts like a
flower in a frost
cover.

*I live
a pathetic
Dean Moriarty,* he

grinned. *You know, the one
who found **it** in the chaos of music & mist
but without his
appetite.*

He
talked and
talked it out in dragon
licks until smoke rose when he paused and
choked on his
sick

no
amount of
words soothed the
dungeon beast from his malignant mental
trap.

*I live
like a shadow,*
he said. *So I'm just
gonna lie here until my candle*

burns to the ground with

Xanax
and firewater
at my feet; don't worry,
he assured me, as I watched like a rabbit
in a snare, *I'll be out of it by spring in a heart-*
beat.

Taxis to Nowhere

I have to go! I have to go where I feel most happy & right now here isn't it. IT is _____ (depending on his fixation, IT could be Italy, Florida, California to name a few). He staggered into the taxi & gave me a reassuring wink with one of his black eyes. We watched him clutch a brown paper bag so taut I couldn't help but think of Linus & his blue blanket. Funny, he was cast as Charlie Brown in his eighth-grade school play. He reached down to scratch his left ankle bloated with a sandwich bag of secret Sweetarts. I knew he was checking to make sure it was still there. *I'm alright! I won't do anything stupid. Believe me.* As the taxi sped off for the third time in two days, we turned toward the house like zombies.

Ischia

> The mind is its own place, and in itself, can make heaven of Hell, and a hell of Heaven. – John Milton

Drifting through Italy's
cobblestone streets,
he faced Ischia again
in a small, shadowy café.

She coiled his tongue
like ivy slipping
down his throat faster
than he could inhale.
The delicacy of her taste
at a moment of compulsion
debilitated his godliness.
She was volcanic and
made him feel mortal.

The café lights went dim.
Damn, could it be this long into the night?
Please, just one more, he begged then promised.
Just one and I swear I'll be over you.
Ischia offered her flavor to his lips

not once but three times over.
She maddened his mind
over and above the exotic
maenad hangers-on
he tasted in Neapolitan cafés
night after night;
they flocked to him,
followed
 him
more than they pursued Adonis,
even the married ones, but
he failed to notice them.

So they left for the water
and threw their thyrsi into the sea.
Saltwater splashed back onto their soft,
livid lips as they vowed never to speak
to him again; they grew weary of his
cyclical temperament.

Lost under Mount Epomeo's vineyard slopes,
they rolled under sheets of green –
Ischia fed him her grapes one by one
in the sweltering Mediterranean sun.

His beard grew homeless;
his nails extended like raven's claws.
He caged Ischia to his chest so tightly
she burst between his covetous grip,
spraying shards of her glass skin through the air
cutting his wrists with deep lacerations.

*What have I done; why
am I bleeding?* He groaned,
as he lay quiescent linked to vines
that dripped life back into his body.

He couldn't remember.

Merciful maenads returned
to their Bacchus like devoted
disciples; they surrounded his bed
trusting their seductive smiles
and Revlon blackened eyes
possessed the charm to convert him.

I am done with her, he avowed
as he did many times before resting
his hand on his chest as if to pledge
allegiance to his promise this time.

His claws reached above his left nipple
to scratch an itch over an ornately inscribed
tattoo injected ten years ago:
"Clear my head
 Stay sober
 The soul controller."
He read these words like Braille
and sighed to the gods,
*Why have I lost the power to control her? I lay buried
like Typhon under her grip.*

The Neighbors

Mother's mood
swings four seasons.
Father's forest fire rages.
Son doesn't set.
Daughter's paisley dress
goads them in a dance.
Pulling down the shade,
their sideshow closes
for the evening.

Chicken Soup
For Erik

his girlfriend dropped him / on a whim / he sat still on his SMA Natas / defying the wheels underneath / Belgian blocks bordered his sweaty back / he stomped on his wet reflection with his left Madrid Fly / tears filled the cracks in the mirror / the pluviophile in me welcomed the precipitation / I sat close to him & shared the puddle / socks on the grass / we waded together / savoring the salty rain on our lips / it tasted just right / I stirred his back with my hand / sister-like / always sister-like / he rested his head on my shoulder / he was seventeen then going on seven / warm in my chicken soup.

The Way I Was

when I sat as a sideliner observing the renegades
pushing around Astor Place like a swarm of
sweaty ants thirsting around a sugar cube.
Hot days & hot nights, pushing & pushing
skating switch until a triumphant roll away
shouted in slow motion, "Ahhh! Doooope!"

The way I was when I noticed a few
had stopped pushing, picked like
ripe papayas for the Kids movie,
while the Washington Square Park pack
kept pushing for a shred of mastery
seen in *Trilogy* or *20 Shot Sequence*.

The way I was when they listened to
Wu-Tang's violins & sword tongues;
Wu steered their impetus to look smooth
like Keenan Milton but Gino's grand Genius
entrance in all its ghostly vapors, haunted
their subconscious in the end.

The way I was when I fled the pushing –
a seeker on a mission banging the concrete
like he who *Casts No Shadow*, strutting
in Clark Wallabees on misty velvet mornings
spiraling down the road like an ancient
Celtic ruin. I wandered & pushed
through Birmingham and London
en route to The Monarch for all-nighters,
grinning in sympathy for the devil.

The way I was when we dressed
like a pack of Pam Coursons and
Ian Browns stomping in evangelical
worship to a '60s mod revival;
Paul tapped his Clarks to the beat
banging his drums better than Baker;
and on we went to Snobs
in Birmingham City Centre
for another all-nighter banging
worn wooden floors when Dan
vomited in front of a cab
and Emma dexterously rubbed

his back while holding two pork pies.
The way I was when I left England
mocking time while regaining it
crossing the Atlantic never supposing
the day would come when the joke
would be on me, 2016 style:
A mortgage, an arduous 9 to 5,
auto-pay sucking the teat of my bank account;
and here I sit listening to Syd sing
it's no good trying struggling to understand
the sequin fan that sped life to where *when*
clings like static to The Way I Was.

The Day After

A tremor & a shift,
Kerouac's *Desolation Pops* dropped
to my feet by the jolt.

Black tea dyed crescents on the envelope,
tsunamis rushed ashore. My heart
raced & read, reread & raced through

your words with a flux capacitor.
Your letter came today, but
we gathered yesterday

by the flowers during
your calling hours. I thought
you never responded.

The White Building
For Gino Iannucci

It was *the* place: Islands,
manuals, waxed curbs, ledges,
drops & pothole deficient
asphalt.
A hum of bees swarmed
menacing & echoing off
of its parking garage walls.
I could hear the vibrations
from across the street
sitting in Gino's Pizzeria.
I crossed back
over the road when
it was safe. As a spectator,
this bevy caused a rumpus
on most weekends.

Over time, metal posts
were planted on the
ledges like King Kong
cages to keep them out,
a subtle reminder from
the authorities: *you are*

the humans & not the beasts.
A sign went up shortly after:
Private Property: No skateboarding
permitted on the premises.
The White Building was no longer
the place, just a fabled
spot among 21st century
skateboarders,
a place where the New York
pro-skaters of the 1990s
got their start.

Twenty-five years later, my
brother, one of the pros,
went back to the White Building
to conduct a video interview
for a skateboarding magazine.
As the cameras rolled & he
pushed to conjure a
back lipslide ghost, a man
in a gray suit stopped the roll:
This is private property. You're
not supposed to be here.
And so he left with
a smile on his face.

Target Rock, 1983

We belly-flopped to the ground,
rolling over stabbing crabgrass
in fits of summer laughter
one eye open with caution for
the coiled ones,
the crooked ones

but we gazed up
at wild blackberry vines
crawling along railroad ties
Mother picked those blackberries
one by one
warming her tongue
with bursts of sweet seeds;
it was easy to forget
when we gazed up

& when she smiled,
toiling soil, whistling
at the clouds staging coups,
inhaling the noon air –

forgetting ourselves,
forgetting the dark
ground creatures
collecting our particles
on their tongues,
flicking reminders
like snapping fingers,
we looked down
weeds dropping
to the hot ground

Father descended
like St. Patrick
to cast them out
across the field
down a sandy sump
running with a lump
in our throats,
we knew then
our little hands
were next in line
to take up the rake
& push those demons out
beyond Target Rock.

Diggum

You stood a fixed mountain
in Radagast's muddy coat & hat –
stone gusts struck your pockets black
& they bled, bled petals & sepals.
Kids sneered as they aimed hitting your
hands while you dug in deep, digging to
feel the flowers as sick perverts do.

They called you *Diggum*.

You swayed like a willow dropping
petals from your pants at the intersection
of Maple & Post, just when school let out.
You watched civilization in an Alice delirium
as cars rubbernecked to see your sideshow.
Crossing guards ushered children away
but I broke free.

I followed you walking alongside
the shadows that clawed the wood.
Did you see me, *Diggum*?
Did you hear tiny steps snap twigs?

O, how I wanted to know, wanted
to see & when I saw you swaying deep
in the wood I understood.

kneeling before a lone stone marker,
groping a pocket for petals,
you carried this load to your *Beloved Son* –
a vacant title etched & exposed – your
name lost under a moss's rug of green –
but am I any better than the stone throwers?
In telling your tale with dolor,

I call you *Diggum.*

Go-Go Boots

You sat white-lipped, pearl-shimmer clouds
below lightning bolted eyebrows.
Twiggy thin, legs crossed in a provocative
pretzel twist with a White Russian in your grip.

Mod fringe, aloof & innocent, you had no
idea who the man was sitting to your right.
I can't think of his name now; was it Emile?
You asked as if I'd know; you were

an antelope in his eyes, fixed & hunted,
but *you* wore the boots, black Go-Go boots,
a follower of Zod, *feminine mystique* aplomb;
your second-wave head turned to face the camera,

undaunted. I can't get over those boots;
they reached your thighs. No wonder the guys
sat neglected to your right . Oh! The parties
you attended. I think the phrase

wearing a lampshade was conceived at this one
when dad felt the mosquito sting off Cam Ranh Bay's
waterways, boots wet in Asian sand as black
& formidable as the Go-Go in your boots,

twisted by the man to your right; he read
your letter & tore the photo. In 1971, it flew back
with him in fragments & all that remains is a
patched-up Kodak with your left boot missing –

the man to your right was saved; my dad was a hero.

Vicious Cycle

When our eyes met for the first time,
I heaved a sigh that I thought you heard.
You knew a simple *hello* and *goodbye* would never
do, so I dropped my weighty anchor into your palm
and you rubbed it seven times like a horseshoe.

When our eyes met for the second time,
I picked your words like berries while catching
chords that fell from your guitar strings; my arms
were open like a basket eager to carry your
lyrics as if they were meant for me.

When our eyes met for the third time,
it was in a delirious dream of whirling desert sand.
Yellow & tan, tan & yellow scenes of grit crusting
my sight, distorting your fair face like an omen; you
were a dark creature choking in a harmonica neck hold.

When our eyes met for the fourth time,
Alex Forrest gazed back at me on the edge
of psychosis sinking in paranoia quicksand
with arms flailing, gasping for air,
suffocating in your circle of games.

When our eyes met for the fifth time,
I willingly closed them; hoisted my anchor from
your palm and walked into the woods like an
emancipated slave where Anath took me in;
she placed a bow and sickle in my hand so

when our eyes meet for the sixth time,
I will have the skills and weapons to resist you;
And it will be you who will heave
a sigh that will go unheard
at the sight of me – strong and dauntless.
But the day will come when you will hum

another song that will break me
and the vicious cycle between us
will resuscitate, rendering us helpless-
gyrating like a *red and yellow mane
on a stallion horse.*

Note: Anath is a Canaanite warrior Goddess, the maiden who loves battle, and known as the virgin Goddess of sacrifice, a warrior and archer.

Wild Woman

I love my wild woman!
he said
in his relaxed
sultry voice
like a 1960s
rock star.
she *was* feral
like Woodstock &
Studio 54 combined,
flaunting
a studded
neck choker –

inside a domestic cage,
ensnared like a
hunted rabbit,
strangled by a
short leash
of mind twists.

he aimed to save her
pulling at the iron bars

from the outside
like Harry Houdini-
a wild man & wild woman,
made from the same magic.

he knew
that muted
psychological torment
was more destructive than
overt aggression

& she howled
at the realization,
trying to escape
with his coaching-
he pulled & pulled,

but she knew then,
wiping the sweat
from his face,
it was all an illusion.
she was the only one
who could set herself
free.

Ophelia's Stepsister

She was a bonnie little brunette
with wilting harebell eyes
blushing a Blake Innocence –
an innocence shared and aired
through woodwinds and strings,
inhaled in ale and bannocks
strewn together in a
whimsical, besotted
tapestry she stitched
behind stone walls.
They had their surreptitious ritual
beneath the north Romanesque window;
fragmented light slashed their bodies
in an otherwise aphotic alcove
where he learned to kiss,
she learned to feel; two adolescents
intoxicated by fallacious spirits.
She thought he was true.
Why wouldn't she?
He had hands so irresistibly
tender in all their stable-worn
roughness and a ginger scruff
that abraded her elegant skin

whispering tales of devotion.
She was drawn to his cyclical temperament,
his egocentric air of morose mood drifts
that begged, *figure me out. I'm so worth it
if you could just figure me out.*
He took her
downstream
with him
as if to test her,
examine her
like a suspected witch:
Will she sink or float?
She followed him willingly as
Thoreau walked deliberately
into Walden wood.
And there she will
wander in her 10´ x 15´
toxic habitat until
she can decipher the
difference between
fixation and
love.

Castlerigg Circle

A howling sound of sorrow
wound around each stone
surged by the blow of the
great northern wind,

echoing in remembrance
of a tradesman's aching

breath, a Neolithic gasp
that exhaled from primeval
lungs in heated, penetrative
spirals encircling his maiden's
long, moss-scented neck;
he pursued her silken hair
like a Rapunzel trail through
busy Beltane trade gatherings.

One year he constructed a
small platform of wood & stone
in the center of Castlerigg's
bustling fair on which his maiden
would dance and sing for all
the days of the gathering,

a performance he stopped to watch
before bartering his chisel and scraper.

Year after year after year
he paused to see her
graceful spin atop
his stone like a wind-up
music box, around, around,
and around until the gatherings
Ceased and the two

disappeared
only to resurrect, transformed
in an excavation of
rubble language spoken
in dust, axe head, and bone.
Learned linguists pen specious
tales of Druid altars and
virgin sacrifices ruled by the
mood of the moon.

In vain
The winds off of Thirlmere

and Helvellyn endeavor
to disclose the unsung truth
of a tradesman, his stone stage,
and his beautiful maiden performer.

Raven

Into her
mouth
dropped
his black feather
tickling her throat
with his carrion,
cawing as he
went down

Sea Bush

She pulled
back black
seaweed,
licking her lips.

one strand
caught
between
his lashes,
blinding
him in
sand
& salt.

his face
wilted as
she bucked
a mako shark
aggression in
flash floods
of free shots.

he consumed
her like
seal even
now when her
curls coiled in
gray sea hags.

her back
rubbed against
smashed shells,
toes floundered
under the
sea floor.

she stood
a Siren
to him –
he, her
Poseidon
still thirsty
for her
aged pussy.

Sex in the Sky

I was on my way to Emily Dickinson's house,
when these two clouds spit on my skin.
The storm left them behind, so
they followed me up I-91 North
en route to Amherst.

I soon forgot about the clouds
When I saw you –
you straddled above me
like sex in the sky.
The clouds grew bitter.
They wanted you,
wanted to be part of you,

part of something magnificent
again, & so they ate you out,
stuffed each layer of your promises
into their mouths & took the credit.

I wanted to catch
you – have one more look,
so I tapped on my breaks

to decelerate the race
between us. It was too late.
I watched as they
devour you fast & wild:

They peeled off your *red* cloak
consuming the pain of wars dripping
in your juice mid-chew like komodo dragons.

They pulled at your *orange* slip
then masticated with their mouths open
overriding years of corporate greed
like a fire-eater at the Greatest Show on Earth.

Your *yellow* skin made them howl
in wolf packs as they struggled with
the "peel here" corner; they rubbed
& rubbed until you separated;
the wait was worth it.
You melted in their mouths
like lemon drops soothing
the parasites of addiction.

Your *green* eyes cleansed
their palate like ginger as
they turned over the Earth,
foiling centuries of forest fires.

They drank your *blue* sweat
like boilermakers cleansing
the seas of oil spills in one pint-glass.

Integrity was almost restored
as they sucked the sweetness
from your *indigo* lips.
You made their tongues turn purple
before they went for your *Violet*.

Poor *Violet*!

She was your final layer of hope,
and just like that you were gone –
consumed. The sky wiped their
mouths clean of your candy
as I made a right turn
onto Main Street.

Cattails

Bobbing heads in tune
Under spotlights – rock n' roll
Cattails sway in sunlight.

My Love in Ring Years

I spoke to you
in omens,
held your veiny
hands; warned you.

I watched you
drain chlorophyll
from your skin;
I raked death
in the cold
& buried
it for you.

I stroked your
elephant skin,
weathered &
carved
in Croatoan
codes by
roving lovers
who fucked
at your
feet.

I kissed your
piculet
mutilations
after they
tapped in
black cloaks
so rhythmically,
so savagely
& then
sucked
the living
sap out of
your body.

I loved you
more than
those who lusted
& you trusted
me –

*Why didn't you
listen?*

I smother those
I love.

My teeth sawed
you in pieces;
I cut you down
& reconstructed your
broken self into
a Wicker Man
statue in
my shed.

I counted
our years
together
through your rings,
which I couldn't see
until I saw beneath
your tender cambium.
You loved me
for so long,

and I felt no remorse.
I carried you inside
to the cast iron fire

& threw you in,
one by one.

And as you
struggled to speak
in spit & crack,
I consumed
you still,
inhaling your
last maple-scented
breath.

My Trees at Dusk

This year, I am grateful.
It's the year of alfalfa.
I can walk the field to you;
see you-
a simple task I cannot do
in times of corn.
It's been five years too long.
I follow the thin trail I've worn
breathing in the petrichor.
Your musk! Oh
your scent at dusk
vibrates within me like
a band of crickets.
Your figure grows fierce
against the setting sun.
some say they turn
a flank of towering trolls
while calling *me*
Vanessa Ives for
loving you
like this –
but *this* is the hour!

And so I walk faster.
I approach your muscular
roots & bow like a fool
under your crown.
Oh how I love the way
you take me in
shaking ravens from your limbs
in preparation for my climb.
The warm wind rustles
your hair around my shoulders
& we fall back
into the black
of the silhouette hour
cursing the corn
for separating us.

Hydrangeas

Two knights
stand sentry,
sworn protectors,
rooted to the Earth
of Pinewoods fortress.

Wooden falchions
raised and intertwined,
brothers in arms
dagger the sky –

a warning
to the Cardinals
about to descend
in sermon:
None shall pass.

Helmet snowballs
bow and bend –
a *stand at ease* order
from their queen
as I water

their roots
and prune
their armor
for June's
solstice crusade.

Asintmah's Warning

You can cut me back
in bales of disregard with
your sickle hands and saw grin,
but I am persistent. I will keep

rambling towards you, crawling
on all fours like a masochistic girlfriend
who is begging for your attention
hoping, for once, you will see me

For who I truly am, but
those eyes of yours will
roll over blank, mid-bite
like a sharks eyes as they

have done for centuries in
foolish perceived domination.
I am your breath; I give you
nourishment; you drink from my lips

but I will tell you this: Once worn
and ornery my reedy arms will

shackle your feet through
concrete cracks and pull you down.

Your beard will descend to greet
me as a white flag flaps in defeat;
in time, you will molder in the peat
and your dust will cover the backs

of hypnotic crickets that will detach
your soul in synchronized wing vibrations
in melodies that will scatter and gather
in the thicket then reawaken

a wise raven.

Note: In Athabaskan mythology, Asintmah is an earth and nature goddess; the first woman on Earth.

Howling

Your voice was Velvet Asity
bathing in dust / hymns that
turned
    my ring.

I switched your pitch
in witch's laughs, a bitch
devouring your syllables
    drinking your verse,

gluttonous for your words,
a greedy Nancy Spungen;
you flew & now
    your hum haunts.

I've made deals with God
swapped chords with nature,
battled storms
    in maiming jousts,

rinsed rain through my hair
dripping your songs in settled air-

a repentance.
    Oh!

To hear your voice again!
I'd come
  Howling,
    knocking my
    knuckles through
      the glass.

Note: *Knocking…knuckles through the glass* is from Bronte's "Wuthering Heights"

Women of the 16th Century

As they watched,
A course braid rings her neck
like a string of pearls.
A board releases below...

D
R
O
P

Weight let go

Head in place
An ashen face

A curtain caught in a current
sways-
　side to side

Listen...

A creaky whine
speaks
through frictional
wood and twine.

An Ode to Aurora

You summon *me*, the Night,
in *my* demesne to pierce my *heart of darkness!*
In prism-dewdrop time, you warm me,
tenderly, with phosphorescent blues
with sirens from the sea; you radiate
melodies in a conspiratorial game and
I am your prey like stupid Mercutio –
you make *worms' meat of me.*

You kiss me like Judas with lustrous lips
while Nyx looks on paralyzed by your
renewed charms, by your silken hair,
and your radiant eyes. Oh, how I hate you!
What a fool I am! I am like black vinyl
skipping and spinning the same track
under your nail, but your scratch
feels so good on my back as I reenter

Your chariot to feel its red velvet seats
bespattered with blackberry mucilage
from prior nocturnal retreats. The roses
you spread at my feet are laden with woody thorns,
a medieval trap pressed against my knees.

I am a caged beast, a mere pet in your delicate hands,
hands that raise the dawn like Lazarus whilst
I briefly rest inside your soporific snare.

Illusionist

Larruping his limbs
Repeatedly – an illusionist
Firefly flees a window.

Acknowledgements

I want to thank all those who encompass the Wood: Nature (the wilds of Brunswick County, N.Y.), magical realms (yes, they do exist, just watch the corners of your world for them), the Long Island/NYC skateboarding community, My brother, Gino Iannucci, My mother, Maureen (who put the Byrne in my name), My father, Big Sal, my wider family in the U.S. and in Europe, Kate Garrett, James H. Duncan, Sam Mastandrea aka Sammo, and Cliff Bleidner at Performance Poets Association of Long Island, and Dan Lee.

I am also grateful to publications where some of these poems first appeared: *Three Drops from a Cauldron, Bop Dead City, Red Wolf Journal, Typehouse Literary Magazine, Gargoyle, Mirror Dance, and Rose Red Review, Fickle Muses*, and *Three Line Poetry*. And I can't thank Michael McInnis (Nixes Mate) enough for soliciting work from me and making this book a reality.

About the Author

Nancy Byrne Iannucci is a historian who teaches history and lives poetry in Troy, NY. Her work is published/forthcoming in numerous publications including *Bop Dead City, Allegro Poetry Magazine, Gargoyle, Autumn Sky Poetry Daily, Typehouse Literary Magazine, Riggwelter Press, Poetry Breakfast, Three Drops from a Cauldron, Picaroon Poetry, Hobo Camp Review, Dying Dahlia Review* to name a few. *Temptation of Wood* is her first published poetry collection.

Nixes Mate Books features small-batch artisanal literature, created by writers that use all 26 letters of the alphabet and then some, honing their craft the time-honored way: one line at a time.

Other or Forthcoming Nixes Mate titles:
WE ARE PROCESSION, SEISMOGRAPH | Devon Balwit
ON BROAD SOUND | Rusty Barnes
JESUS IN THE GHOST ROOM | Rusty Barnes
CAPP ROAD | Matt Borczon
HE WAS A GOOD FATHER | Mark Borczon
THE WILLOW HOWL | Lisa Brognano
A WORLD WHERE | Paul Brookes
SHE NEEDS THAT EDGE | Paul Brookes
SQUALL LINE ON THE HORIZON | Pris Campbell
MY SOUTHERN CHILDHOOD | Pris Campbell
FOR LACK OF CALLING | Mark DeCateret
A FIRE WITHOUT LIGHT | Darren C. Demaree
LABOR | Lisa DeSiro
KINKY KEEPS THE HOUSE CLEAN | Mari Deweese
AIR & OTHER STORIES | Lauren Leja
HITCHHIKING BEATITUDES | Michael McInnis
SMOKEY OF THE MIGRAINES | Michael McInnis
I WISH FRANCISCO FRANCO WOULD LOVE ME | Gloria Mindock
THE LIVES OF ATOMS | Lee Okan
LUBBOCK ELECTRIC | Anne Elezabeth Pluto
STARLAND | Jessica Purdy
WAITING FOR AN ANSWER | Heather Sullivan
COMES TO THIS | Jeff Weddle
HEART OF THE BROKEN WORLD | Jeff Weddle
NIXES MATE REVIEW ANTHOLOGY 2016/17

nixesmate.pub/books

www.ingramcontent.com/pod-product-compliance
Lightning Source LLC
Chambersburg PA
CBHW070439010526
44118CB00014B/2116